THE OFFICIAL
CELTIC ANNUAL
2005

Written by
Douglas Russell

g

A Grange Publication

ISBN 1-902704-74-6

£6.99

CONTENTS

CELTIC

THE MANAGER

MARTIN O'NEILL

With the SPL crown for period 2003/04, manager Martin O'Neill celebrated his third title success in just four seasons. The Scottish Cup also returned to Celtic Park, making it a total of six (out of a possible twelve) domestic trophies to date during his period in charge. Martin O'Neill was also voted Manager of the Year by the Scottish Football Writers' Association - for the second time in four years.

THE PLAYERS

RAB DOUGLAS

After starting the first four games of last season, Rab Douglas was rested for the league game against Dundee United at Celtic Park. His replacement in goal, Magnus Hedman, then started nineteen out of the next twenty – two matches both home and abroad before Douglas was back between the sticks when Jim Duffy's Dundee made a pre-Christmas SPL visit to Glasgow in mid-December. Just over one week later, the Scotland goalkeeper more than earned his win bonus when, with Celtic leading 1-0 against Motherwell at Fir Park, he produced a quite magnificent save with his left-hand and clawed away Adams' well-hit penalty kick. Including the Motherwell game, a series of five clean sheets were then recorded with players of both Rangers and Hearts failing to beat him during that period. His fine vein of form continued week-in, week-out and Douglas was an ever-present in the team until he was sensationally red-carded in the tunnel as the players of Celtic and Barcelona left the field at half time in the March Uefa Cup game in Glasgow. The keeper's next game was Championship Day at Rugby Park in mid-April. The following month, a few days before Celtic's Scottish Cup final date with Dunfermline, Douglas underwent surgery in England to finally cure a long-term thigh problem.

DAVID MARSHALL

In late March, aged just 19 years and three weeks, the young Scottish goalkeeper produced a man-of-the-match performance in the Uefa Cup game with Barcelona at the Nou Camp Stadium. Marshall, standing in for the suspended Rab Douglas, was simply awesome as he defied the Spanish giants with a series of wondrous stops in the 0-0 draw as Celtic progressed to the quarter-final stage of last season's competition. In January the previous year, after having signed professional terms in 2002, he made his first-team debut in the third round of the Scottish Cup when Javier Sanchez Broto was injured during the tie with St. Johnstone. Progress to the starting line-up was achieved in December 2003 when Marshall was a member of the side that defeated Partick Thistle 2-0 at Firhill in the third round of the CIS Insurance Cup. The day after his heroic Barcelona display, it was confirmed that the young man had signed a lucrative new four year contract with Celtic. On the Sunday of that same week, David Marshall was deservedly voted BBC Scotland's Man of the Match following the Old Firm clash with Rangers when he again produced some quite astonishing saves to defy the home side. Apart from SPL Championship Day at Rugby Park in April, the young man was then an ever-present in the team up to and including the last game of the campaign at Hampden in May.

JOOS VALGAEREN

In a stop-start injury jinxed season, the Belgian-born defender was in the starting line-up for the first six games of the 2003/04 campaign. The stopper was then out of action right up until late October and the Champions League encounter in his homeland against Anderlecht when he came on as a replacement for Jackie McNamara at the start of the second half. Then, after beginning the next weekend's 4-0 SPL victory over Aberdeen at Celtic Park, Valgaeren was limited to a number of substitute appearances before returning for the start of the Old Firm clash against Rangers in early March when he performed admirably out of position at left-back.

JACKIE McNAMARA

Filling a variety of roles in the team (including that of captain on many notable occasions), Jackie 'Mr Versatile' McNamara had a wonderfully consistent 2003/04 campaign regardless of the position he was detailed to fill by manager Martin O'Neill. It is surely worth noting that the player, who never lets anyone down, appeared at right-back, left-back, right wing-back as well as in midfield or as one of three central defenders at different times last season! It came as no real surprise when he was named as the Scottish Football Writers' Association Player of the Year for Season 2003/04, forty years after another great Celt Billy McNeill had won the first-ever writers' award. Indeed, McNamara was the third Celt in four years to be honoured this way, following in the footsteps of both Paul Lambert and Henrik Larsson. After scoring with a magnificent right-foot drive from the edge of the box in his first appearance last term (5-0 v Dundee United, 16.8.03), McNamara made the starting line-up in sixteen of the next twenty competitive matches both home and abroad. The player, a Tommy Burns signing from 1995, was then an ever-present in the side from the end of December until the end of February's Uefa Cup game with FK Teplice when he filled the left-back position in the 3-0 victory. On the night that Celtic's interest in the aforementioned European tournament ended in Spain, McNamara was again outstanding in defence and could easily have won his side a first half penalty when Villarreal captain Arruabarrena brought him down in the box as he broke for a Larsson flick. Towards the end of last season, it was confirmed that the player had agreed a welcome contract extension to the summer of 2005.

STANISLAV VARGA

The Slovak defender, whose Uefa Cup performance against Barcelona in the Nou Camp stadium was truly inspirational, was indeed a colossus for Celtic right throughout the 2003/04 campaign. After claiming his first goal of the season during the 5-0 demolition of Hearts at Celtic Park in October, Varga scored with another header the following month when Dunfermline met the same fate in the east end of Glasgow. Although his opener in the December CIS Cup game with Hibernian at Easter Road was not enough to secure victory (1-2, 18.12.03), Celtic fans had good reason to celebrate when his name was on the second of three Old Firm beauties as Rangers were comprehensively beaten 3-0 in early January. Then, on the plastic pitch at Dunfermline the following month, Varga gave his side a 2-1 lead before netting a double in the Firhill clash with Partick Thistle less than two weeks later. This 4-1 triumph saw Celtic stretch their winning league record to 24 games which meant that Morton's 40 year-old record (of 23 consecutive league victories) had finally been surpassed. By the end of the SPL campaign, only Henrik Larsson had started more league encounters, with 36 appearances as opposed to Varga's 35.

RECORD BREAKING CELTIC

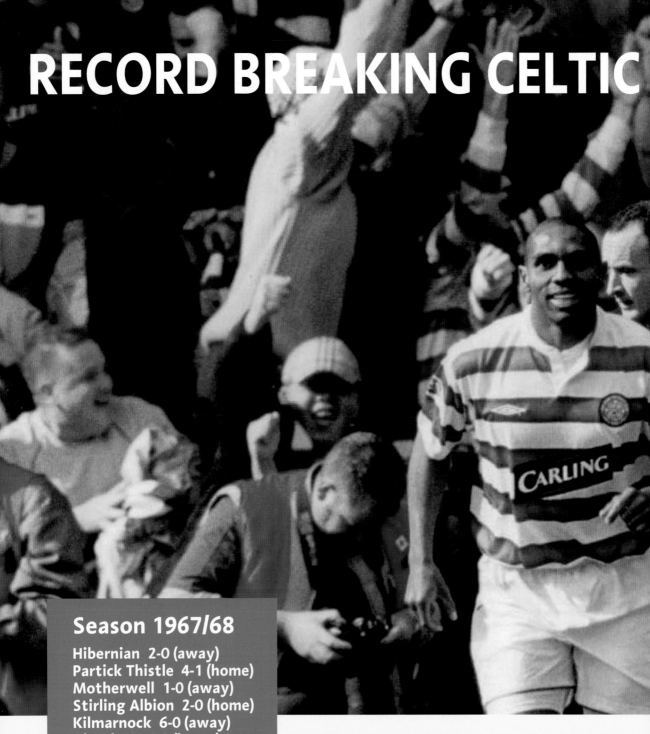

Season 1967/68

Hibernian 2-0 (away)
Partick Thistle 4-1 (home)
Motherwell 1-0 (away)
Stirling Albion 2-0 (home)
Kilmarnock 6-0 (away)
Aberdeen 4-1 (home)
Airdrie 4-0 (away)
Falkirk 3-0 (away)
Raith Rovers 5-0 (home)
St. Johnstone 6-1 (away)
Dundee United 5-0 (home)
Hearts 2-0 (away)
Aberdeen 1-0 (away)
Dundee 5-2 (home)
Morton 2-1 (home)
Dunfermline 2-1 (away)
Season 1968/69
Clyde 3-0 (away)

Martin O'Neill's all-conquering side established a new club record of 18 straight league wins in a row after defeating Rangers at Ibrox in early January 2004. The previous best sequence was back in the late sixties

RECORD BREAKING CELTIC

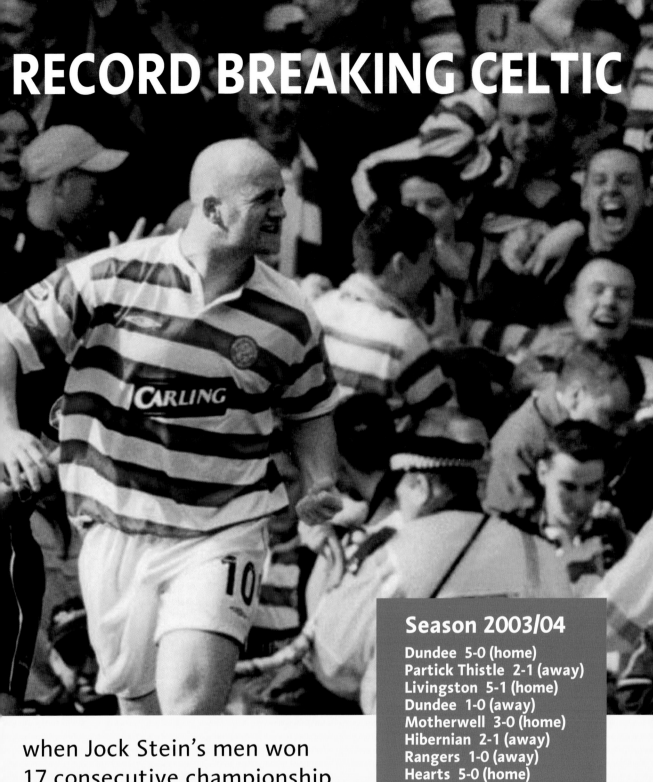

when Jock Stein's men won 17 consecutive championship games before losing to Rangers in the second league game of Season 1968/69. Each winning sequence is detailed here.

Season 2003/04

Dundee 5-0 (home)
Partick Thistle 2-1 (away)
Livingston 5-1 (home)
Dundee 1-0 (away)
Motherwell 3-0 (home)
Hibernian 2-1 (away)
Rangers 1-0 (away)
Hearts 5-0 (home)
Aberdeen 4-0 (home)
Kilmarnock 5-0 (away)
Dunfermline 5-0 (home)
Dundee 5-1 (away)
Partick Thistle 3-1 (home)
Livingston 2-0 (away)
Dundee 3-2 (home)
Motherwell 2-0 (away)
Hibernian 6-0 (home)
Rangers 3-0 (home)

JOHN KENNEDY

Following the youngster's superb March displays in the crucial away games with Barcelona (in the Uefa Cup) and Rangers (in the SPL), Scotland manager Berti Vogts named the tall, confident Kennedy in the national side to play Romania at Hampden the following week in a so-called 'friendly' international. Tragically, after only some fourteen minutes of play, the defender was on the receiving end of a shocking tackle by Wolverhampton's loan Ganea that seriously damaged ligaments in his left knee. This meant that the talented young Bhoy would be out of action until 2005. Kennedy, who has filled the positions of right-back, left-back and centre-half with the same determined assurance, claimed his first goal for the club back in December 2003 when he hit the late winner against Dundee after appearing as substitute for Johan Mjallby in the league encounter at Celtic Park. In early June 2004, it was confirmed that the player had agreed a new two year contract.

BOBO BALDE

Voted Player of the Year in Celtic's inaugural award ceremony two seasons ago, the giant stopper had another magnificently assertive and dominating campaign throughout virtually all of the 2003/04 period. From the word go, he was a true rock at the heart of the defence. In mid-September at Dens Park (game five of the SPL title race), Balde netted the only goal of the game against Dundee when he seemed to rise a couple of feet above everybody else to power home a penalty box header. His second of the season was another headed strike in another league game with Jim Duffy's side but on this occasion over 57,000 fans acclaimed the goal which put Celtic 2-1 ahead in an encounter that would eventually finish 3-2 in favour of the home side. After the SPL capital clash with Hearts at Tynecastle in January 2004, Balde was on international duty with Guinea in the African Nations Cup when his country reached the quarter-final stage of the tournament before being knocked-out by Mali. His first game after returning 'home' was the St. Valentine's Day 2-1 victory over Dundee United at Celtic Park. From then until the end of the season, Balde was his usual impressive self at the heart of the Celtic rearguard.

DAVID FERNANDEZ

The talented Spaniard returned to the squad for Season 2004/05 after spending the previous year away from Celtic Park on-loan to his former club Livingston where he played a major part in their domestic success last term. The West Lothian club not only reached the semi-final of the Scottish Cup (losing 3-1 to Celtic at Hampden) but also famously lifted the CIS Cup after beating Hibernian 2-0 in the final at the National Stadium. As usual, Fernandez was a joy to watch that day.

DIDIER AGATHE

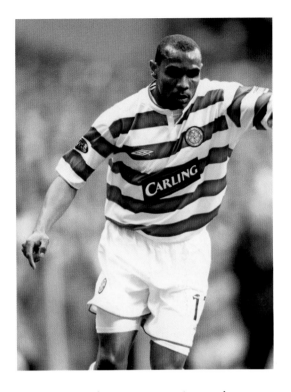

The right wing-back, signed for just £50,000 back in September 2000, had another vintage season both home and abroad. Although the player's name was never on the score sheet at any time in Season 2002/03, after just the fifth game of last term Didier Agathe had already netted twice, with the goals coming in the space of just three days and in consecutive matches. His first strike, the second of the game, was in Budapest when fellow Champions League hopeful's MTK Hungaria were beaten 4-0 before his second (also the second of this particular clash) helped Celtic on the way to a crushing 5-0 triumph over Dundee United in the east end of Glasgow on a blisteringly hot August Saturday. The following month, Agathe was controversially red-carded during the SPL encounter at Dens Park. Then, during the Champions League game with Bayern Munich at Celtic Park in late November, a hamstring problem prematurely ended his involvement in both that and several subsequent matches until the end of the year. The player returned for the crucial Old Firm meeting at the beginning of January (when he successfully nullified the threat of winger Peter Lovenkrands) and, at the end of that same month, claimed his third goal of the campaign which opened the second half flood gates to a memorable 5-1 victory over Kilmarnock. Probably his most memorable goals of the whole campaign were scored in late March and early April with a crucial double at Easter Road against Hibernian (4-0, 21.3.04) and an injury time equaliser against their capital rivals Hearts (2-2, 3.4.04) that maintained Celtic's amazing unbeaten home run of games.

NEIL LENNON

Although the last time Neil Lennon scored for Celtic was back on the very first day of December 2001 when Alex McLeish was manager of the visiting Hibernian, the 34-year-old's worth to the side is much more than even a barrow full of goals to his name. The wee man, who takes up excellent positions around the pitch, is very much a players' player whose immense contribution on a weekly basis to the team is sometimes not always fully appreciated. When Martin O'Neill uses a back three defensive formation, Lennon is usually deployed just in front of the middleman of the threesome (the most vulnerable player in that system) with the Irishman, therefore, performing as an extra stopper or holding midfielder as opposed to 'normal' midfielder. It is worth noting that when Celtic lost at Easter Road in the CIS Cup tournament last season, Lennon, the former Northern Ireland international, was missing from the team. The player capped a tremendous period towards the end of the various campaigns with his award as SPL Bank of Scotland Player of the Month for March 2004 although even this was eclipsed when the fans, some weeks later, confirmed the Irishman as their choice for Celtic Player of the Year, Season 2003/04.

PAUL LAMBERT

Having played in five of Celtic's opening six competitive games last season, Paul Lambert (following a Stilian Petrov cutback) scored the opener against Partick Thistle at Firhill in late August. At the turn of the year, the midfielder claimed his second of the campaign when First Division Ross County came to Glasgow on Scottish Cup duty and returned north following a 2-0 loss.

WHAT THE
PAPERS SAID

CELTIC MADE THE FOLLOWING FOOTBALL HEADLINES DURING SEASON 2003/04.

**WHAT WAS THE OCCASION?
THE CLUE IS IN THE DATE!**

1. 'OUT OF RANGE' Sunday Times, 4.1.04

2. 'SUTTON INSPIRES TURKEY SHOOT'
Sunday Times, 28.12.03

3. 'BHOYS' 21 GUN SALUTE' Sunday Mirror, 1.2.04

4. 'THE BHOY'S GOT HART' Sunday Mirror, 5.10.03

5. 'DOUGLAS RELIES ON STRONG-ARM TACTICS' Daily Mail, 22.12.03

6. 'SWEDE DELIVERS THE LAST RITES' Daily Mail, 8.3.04

7. 'MBE FOR O'NEILL: IT'S MY BEST EVER NIGHT AS MANAGER' Daily Mail, 26.3.04

8. 'AS GOOD AS IT GETS' Daily Mail, 19.4.04

9. 'THE LOST BHOY' Daily Mail, 26.4.04

10. 'FAIRY-TALE ENDING FOR PLAYER WHO IS CLOSE TO PERFECTION' Daily Mail, 17.5.04

ANSWERS ON PAGE 60

CELTIC AND THE DOMESTIC CUPS QUIZ

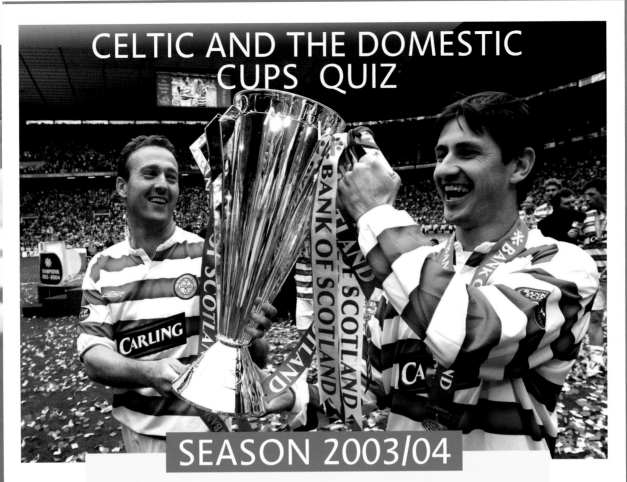

SEASON 2003/04

1. Name their opponents when Celtic entered the Tennent's Scottish Cup campaign at the third round stage in early January 2004.

2. Who kept goal for Celtic in the CIS Cup tie at Firhill in December 2003?

3. What was the result in the above game and who scored for Celts?

4. Who scored for Celtic (at Easter Road) in the quarter-final of the CIS Cup?

5. Hearts finished the February 2004 Scottish Cup tie with ...... men. Fill in the missing number.

6. Name the player who claimed a double in the above game.

7. John Hartson and Chris Sutton both missed the March Scottish Cup clash with holders Rangers. True or false?

8. Whose name was on two of the three Celtic goals when Livingston were beaten 3-0 at the semi-final stage of the Scottish Cup?

9. Henrik Larsson scored Celtic's final goal in the Scottish Cup Final. True or false?

10. Who skippered the team at Hampden that day?

ANSWERS ON PAGE 60

ALAN THOMPSON

Near the end of last season, it was confirmed that the Geordie (the only Celtic midfielder to have scored in consecutive 2003/04 Old Firm league games) had signed a contract extension keeping him at the club until the summer of 2007. This news was just what the fans had hoped for as dead-ball specialist Alan Thompson has, in truth, been a model of consistency for Celtic since Martin O'Neill brought the player to Glasgow from Birmingham back in September 2000. Although it would take far too long to detail the actual number of goals that Thompson created or had a hand in last season, there is enough space to consider those strikes that the prolific midfielder actually converted himself! In late August, he scored in three consecutive SPL games when Dundee United (5-0), Partick Thistle (2-1) and Livingston (5-1) were all beaten. The following month, his goal in the Champions League clash with Bayern Munich in Germany was not enough to avoid defeat (1-2) although his league opener against Hibernian at Easter Road set Celtic on the way to a reversal of the aforementioned score. Thompson then netted in two away championship fixtures when Livingston and Motherwell both lost 2-0 before claiming goal number three on the afternoon when Rangers' faint title hopes were finally extinguished 3-0 at Celtic Park in January. The number three featured again for the midfielder in February. This time, however, it was his total goal tally for the month which comprised one against Dunfermline (on the infamous plastic pitch when rather sensibly he was sporting thick black tights) and a double in the Glasgow joust with Livingston that ended 5-1 to put his side sixteen points clear in the title race. Probably his most celebrated goal of the various campaigns was scored on that emotionally draining night of high drama at Celtic Park in March when the Primera Liga might of Barcelona were a beaten 1-0 side. Three days after the superb 0-0 result in the return leg with Frank Rijkaard's side in Spain, Thompson's last goal of the season was the Old Firm winner when Rangers lost 2-1 at Ibrox.

STILIAN PETROV

The Bulgarian, brought to the club by Kenny Dalglish and John Barnes in the summer of 1999, was yet another player who contributed massively to the success of Season 2003/04 and was one of three Celtic nominations for the Scottish PFA Player of the Year. His first goal of the campaign was number three of four when Celts booked their place in the Champions League group stages following a 4-0 third qualifying round victory over MTK Hungaria in Budapest. Although the fans had to wait until post-Christmas for his next strike, it was at this time that the powerhouse Petrov hit a rich vein of scoring form. The week after the midfielder's goal in the demolition of Hibernian at Celtic Park (6-0, 27.12.03), he netted the crucial Old Firm opener against Rangers at home when the defending SPL Champions were swamped 3-0 and well on the way to losing their league crown. With New Year goals in the subsequent games with Hearts (1-0, 18.1.04) and Aberdeen (3-1, 24.1.04), it meant that Petrov had scored in four consecutive SPL outings. After a week's break, he was back on the goal trail again but this time the competition was the Scottish Cup when his double at Tynecastle (3-0, 7.2.04) played a major part in ending Hearts' interest in the grand old trophy for yet another year. The player's tally for Season 2003/04 so far reached eight in total when his mid-March opener against Dundee at Dens Park set Celtic on the road to an eventual 2-1 triumph. One month later, it was his goal against Kilmarnock at Rugby Park in April that finally confirmed Celtic as SPL Champions with six league games still to play. Petrov then capped a marvellous championship season with his BBC 'Man of the Match' award in the final Old Firm clash of that campaign as Celtic made it six-in-a-row over their greatest rivals. By season's end, the midfielder (who netted his side's third and last goal on Scottish Cup Final Day) was one of only four players to have made over thirty league starts for Celtic. The player then headed for Portugal as captain of his country for Euro 2004.

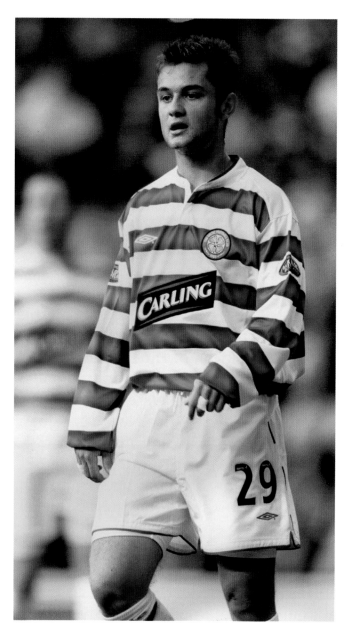

SHAUN MALONEY

The young striker's 2003/04 campaign was brought to a cruel and abrupt end when, during the Under-21 game with Partick Thistle on February 23, he ruptured anterior cruciate ligaments in his left knee. Following subsequent surgery by the eminent Dr Richard Steadman in America, the player returned to Scotland at the end of March to begin his rehabilitation programme which would, understandably, take a considerable amount of time. Last season had started well for Shaun and, after making a substitute appearance, he scored in the first game of that winning period when Kaunus were beaten 4-0 at Celtic Park in the Champions League qualifier. He then netted in three consecutive home SPL encounters when Dundee United (5-0), Livingston (5-1) and Motherwell (3-0) were all put to the sword in the early stages of the league campaign in August and September. At the end of May 2004, it was confirmed that Maloney had signed a new three-year deal with the club.

JOHN HARTSON

The big man's 2003/04 campaign ended prematurely when it was confirmed in early March that he required an operation to resolve an ongoing disc problem in his back. Although not the same disc, it was a similar injury that ruled the player out of the UEFA Cup Final with Porto the previous year. The striker's first goal last season was, of course, the famous winner at Ibrox in early October that put Celtic in the driving seat and helped them overtake league leaders Rangers at the top of the SPL

table. In addition to being the Welshman's 50th goal for the club, it also meant that Hartson had now scored in the past three Old Firm league games with Celtic winning them all by a single goal. Prior to his injury, the striker claimed a total of nine league strikes last term with delightful doubles in the championship clashes with Dunfermline (5-0, 8.11.03), Hibernian (6-0, 27.12.03) and Kilmarnock (5-1, 31.1.04). Although the player returned to full training towards the end of the season, his involvement in the Scottish Cup Final with Dunfermline was sadly never going to be a realistic possibility.

STEPHEN PEARSON

After arriving at Celtic from Motherwell during the January 2004 transfer window, the youngster (Scottish PFA and Scottish Football Writers' Association Young Player of the Year for Season 2003/04) started his first game for the club later that same month when Hearts were beaten 1-0 at Tynecastle, courtesy of a Stilian Petrov goal. He joined the Bulgarian on the list of scorers at Pittodrie one week later, netting from close-in the third of Celtic's three in the 3-1 SPL triumph. When Kilmarnock were demolished 5-1 in Glasgow seven days later, Pearson scored his second Celtic goal with a sweet shot past former team mate Dubordeaux in goal after Neil Lennon's pass. His own personal hat-trick was completed on the last day of February when his opener broke the deadlock against Livingston in another SPL clash (his ninth consecutive appearance) that would eventually also end 5-1 in favour of the league leaders and champions elect. In truth, Stephen Pearson has been a revelation since arriving at Celtic Park.

CHRIS SUTTON

Richly deserving his Scottish PFA Player of the Year award for Season 2003/04, Chris Sutton had been a model of consistency and excelled not only up front but also in midfield as well as defence during that period. No wonder everybody at Celtic Park was delighted when, in April 2004, the player agreed a one year extension to his current contract with the option of a second year, meaning that Sutton would be at the club until the summer of 2006 at least. Due to suspension, Sutton missed the first five SPL games of the 2003/04 campaign but, during that period 'away' from the Scottish League, he was still in a goal-scoring frame of mind and netted in Celtic's European clashes with Kaunas at home (4-0, 30.7.03) and MTK Hungaria in Glasgow and Budapest when Celtic won 4-0 and 1-0 respectively. Following Sutton's first domestic strike in the 3-0 September defeat of Motherwell, the player's subsequent tally included hat-tricks in the 5-0 destruction of Kilmarnock and the 5-1 drubbing of Dundee United (both November SPL outings) as well as crucial goals in the Champions League victories over both Lyon and Anderlecht in September and November respectively. December was another good month and his overall tally increased by four with conversions against Livingston (2-0, 6.12.03), Lyon (2-3, 10.12.03) and a brace in the stunning 6-0 win over Bobby Williamson's Hibernian two days after Christmas. The next time his name appeared as a scorer was on St. Valentine's Day when his late penalty winner in the 2-1 victory over Dundee United ensured no temporary slip-up in the championship race. His 24th of the season (in all competitions) came during the 5-1 thumping of Livingston on the last day of February, just before his 31st birthday. This goal was indeed something of a milestone as it represented number 50 of a rather unique partnership with 'King of Kings' Henrik Larsson. The week after netting in the 2-2 draw with Hearts, he claimed another brace when Livingston were beaten 3-1 in the semi-final of the Scottish Cup at Hampden. However, his last minute strike against Rangers at Celtic Park in the final Old Firm encounter of the season was, for most fans, the moment that lit up the latter stages of the 2003/04 league campaign as well as being a genuine candidate for goal of the season.

KING OF GOALS

HENRIK LARSSON QUIZ

1. Henrik Larsson arrived at Celtic after playing with which European club?

2. Who was Celtic manager at that time?

3. Larsson's first outing for Celtic was against Hibernian at Easter Road. What part did he play in the winning goal that day?

4. The club failed to win any domestic honours by the end of his first season in Glasgow. True or false?

5. How many goals did Larsson score during his second season (1998/99) with Celts?

6. Tragedy struck in October 1999. What happened…where?

7. In 2000/01, Henrik netted fifty times in all competitions. True or false?

8. Name the player whose post-war record of forty-eight goals was finally surpassed in Season 2000/01.

9. Did Larsson score at Celtic Park on Championship Day 2002 when Livingston lost 5-1?

10. Henrik Larsson reached an astonishing 240 goals for the club at Celtic Park on the last day of the SPL campaign in May 2004. Can you name the other two legendary strikers who remain ahead of him in Celtic's goalscoring chart?

ANSWERS ON PAGE 60

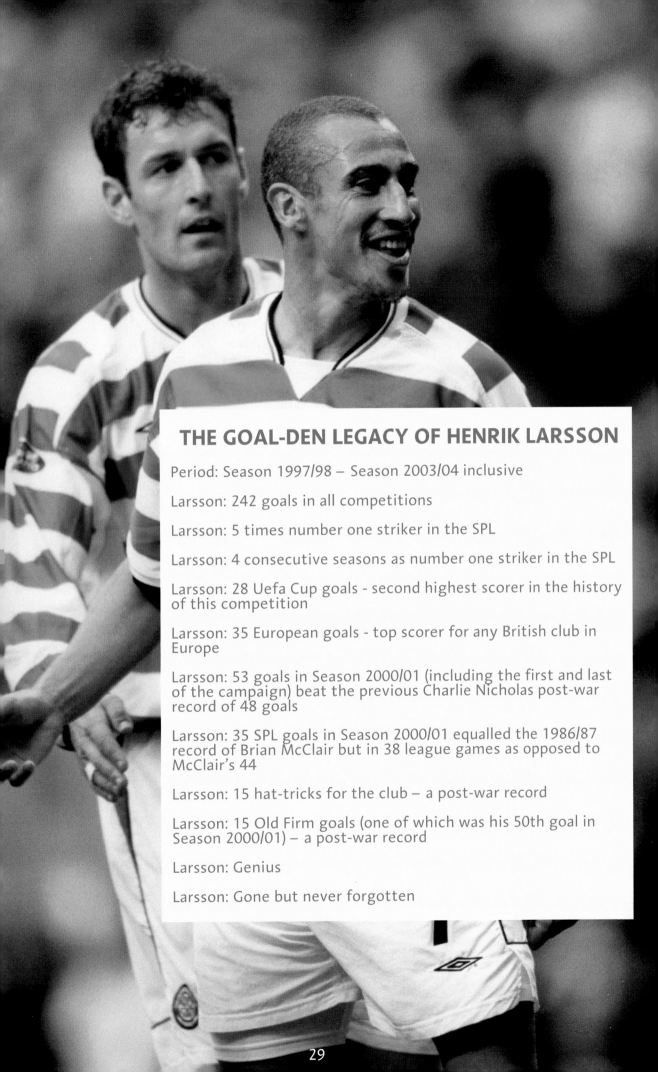

THE GOAL-DEN LEGACY OF HENRIK LARSSON

Period: Season 1997/98 – Season 2003/04 inclusive

Larsson: 242 goals in all competitions

Larsson: 5 times number one striker in the SPL

Larsson: 4 consecutive seasons as number one striker in the SPL

Larsson: 28 Uefa Cup goals - second highest scorer in the history of this competition

Larsson: 35 European goals - top scorer for any British club in Europe

Larsson: 53 goals in Season 2000/01 (including the first and last of the campaign) beat the previous Charlie Nicholas post-war record of 48 goals

Larsson: 35 SPL goals in Season 2000/01 equalled the 1986/87 record of Brian McClair but in 38 league games as opposed to McClair's 44

Larsson: 15 hat-tricks for the club – a post-war record

Larsson: 15 Old Firm goals (one of which was his 50th goal in Season 2000/01) – a post-war record

Larsson: Genius

Larsson: Gone but never forgotten

JOHNNY CRUM'S JERSEY 1938

To mark the importance of the Empire Exhibition of 1938, a prestigious football tournament was organised and featured, amongst other teams, Celtic, Rangers, Chelsea, Everton and Sunderland. Following a 0-0 draw with Sunderland in their first game, Celtic disposed of the team from the north east of England 3-1 after the next evening's replay with Johnny Crum one of the scorers. It was centre-forward Crum himself who netted the only goal of the game in the next round (when Hearts were disposed of 1-0) and propelled the 'Hoops' to a final date with destiny.

With the scalps of both Rangers and Aberdeen already on their belt, the powerful Everton (with ten internationalists from all four home countries at their disposal) stood between Celtic and the trophy. Before some 82,000 spectators on a June afternoon, there was little to separate two quite marvellous sides and it took a solitary goal (in extra-time) to eventually settle the trophy's ultimate destination. The hero of the day was none other that the aforementioned Johnny Crum who scored his third goal in as many games. The trophy was on its way to the east end of Glasgow and a permanent display inside Celtic park where, quite rightly, it has pride of place to this very day.

This is the actual jersey worn by Johnny Crum on Empire Exhibition Final Day.

THIS JERSEY WAS WORN BY JOHNNY CAMP
IN THE EXHIBITION CUP FINAL OF 1930.
JOHNNY SCORED THE WINNING GOAL IN
THE 3-0 DEFEAT OF EVERTON.

CHAMPIONS QUIZ

1. Who scored Celtic's first and last goals of the SPL season?

2. Prior to Christmas last season, the Bhoys netted five times on six separate league occasions. Name the SPL opponents.

3. Can you name the only player who started every SPL game from August until the end of December?

4. Who was the first player to claim a league hat-trick for Celts last term?

5. He claimed the opening goal in the first three league clashes of 2004. Name the Celt.

6. What happened to Bobo Balde after the Tynecastle fixture in January 2004?

7. What was the final score when Celtic played on Dunfermline's synthetic surface for the first time last season?

8. Whose name was on Celtic's 50th home SPL goal of the campaign?

9. Who scored the winner when league title number 39 was celebrated at Rugby Park in mid-April?

10. What was extremely unusual about the next league encounter?

ANSWERS ON PAGE 61

SEASON 2003/04
OLD FIRM QUIZ

1. What was the score in the first Old Firm game of the season?

2. Name the player who scored the winner that day.

3. What was unusual about Celtic's opening goal in the 3-0 January triumph at Celtic Park?

4. Who captained the side for this game?

5. How many points were Celtic clear at the top of this SPL after this encounter?

6. John Hartson claimed his 40th goal for Celtic in the first Old Firm clash of the season. True or false?

7. Who scored for Celtic in the March Scottish Cup game against Rangers?

8. When Henrik Larsson opened the scoring at Ibrox in the March league encounter, it was Old Firm goal number ..... for him. Fill in the missing number.

9. Who scored the winner in the above clash?

10. Name the player whose last minute strike in the final Old Firm clash of the season ensured six-in-a-row victories over Rangers.

ANSWERS ON PAGE 61

POLAR BEAR TROPHY 1975

The season after Celtic's historic 'nine-in-a-row' run of consecutive championship wins finally ended, the club appeared in the European Cup Winners' Cup of 1975/76 and faced Valur of Iceland in the opening round of the competition.

When the sides lined-up to face each other in the first leg in Iceland, it was interesting to note that the brother of Celtic's Icelandic player 'Shuggie' Edvaldsson was also on the park - in the colours of Valur. Guess which brother was smiling when the Celtic man managed to miss a twice-taken penalty that night? Despite this double blunder, the visitors still returned south to Scotland having achieved a good 2-0 away victory after goals from Wilson and MacDonald.

Two weeks later, the suggestion that the return leg would be nothing more than a formality was confirmed when Celtic cruised to a 5-0 advantage before half time. With two additional strikes in the second period of the game, the seven goals were split amongst six players with Harry Hood, having claimed a double, the odd man out.

Just like the unfortunate seal in this rather bizarre Icelandic gift, Valur had met a similar fate…..and been devoured by the beast that was Celtic!

16.9.75   VALUR 0 CELTIC 2
                          Wilson (7 mins)
                          MacDonald (74 mins)

Celtic: Latchford, McGrain, Lynch, McCluskey, MacDonald, Edvaldsson, Hood (Glavin), McNamara, Dalglish, Callaghan and Wilson.

1.10.75   CELTIC 7 VALUR 0
                          Edvaldsson (6 mins)
                          Dalglish (12 mins)
                          P. McCluskey (30 mins)
                          Hood (37, 82 mins)
                          Deans (42 mins)
                          Callaghan (50 mins)

Celtic: Latchford, McGrain, Lynch, P. McCluskey, MacDonald, Edvaldsson, Wilson (G. McCluskey), Dalglish, Deans, Callaghan (Casey) and Hood.

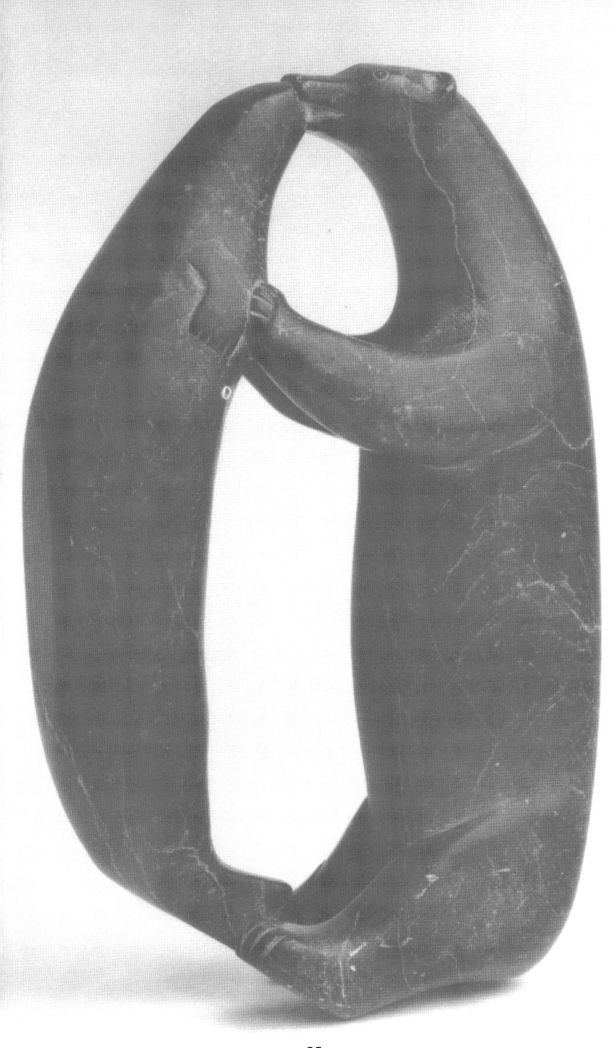

When Celtic defeated Rangers in the last Old Firm clash of Season 2003/04, Martin O'Neill's side extended their consecutive run of victories to six games over their greatest rivals. For a similar record of continuous Old Firm wins, you would have to return to the years of 1971 and 1972 when the legendary Jock Stein was manager of the club.

PAST GLORY

Celtic 2 Rangers 1 Scottish Cup Final Replay, May, 1971

This was a double season of League and Scottish Cup triumph for Celtic. After a 1-1 drawn game, they triumphed 2-1 in the final replay of the Scottish Cup when goals from Lou Macari and Harry Hood delighted at least half of the 103,000 spectators at Hampden.

Celtic 2 Rangers 0 League Cup, August 1971

In the League Cup section stage, late goals from Jimmy Johnstone and Old Firm debutant Kenny Dalglish ensured a straight-forward victory. Although officially a home tie, this game was actually played at Ibrox as Celtic Park was under reconstruction at the time.

Rangers 0 Celtic 3 League Cup, August 1971

The 'return' leg in the same League Cup competition and Celtic were even more convincing with Kenny Dalglish, Tom Callaghan and Bobby Lennox all on the score-sheet at Ibrox.

Rangers 2 Celtic 3 League Championship, September 1971

Despite being behind 2-1 at one stage, a last minute Jimmy Johnstone header meant full points for the visitors. Lou Macari and Kenny Dalglish (again) were the other Celtic scorers.

Celtic 2 Rangers 1 League Championship, January 1972

Another late headed goal secured victory but this time it was from the head of Jim Brogan. 'Jinky' Johnstone (whose name was on the opener in the east end of Glasgow that day) and his team-mates were now well on the way to seven-in-a-row title flags.

Celtic 3 Rangers 1 League Championship, September, 1972

Another season - another victory! Celtic were coasting 3-0 after goals from Kenny Dalglish, Jimmy Johnstone and Lou Macari put them on easy street before Greig netted for Rangers in the last minute of play.

PRESENT GLORY

Rangers 1 Celtic 2 League Championship, April 2003

Only some seventy-two hours after confirming their place in the UEFA Cup final, Celtic headed for Ibrox on league duty in the latter days of Season 2003/04. Alan Thompson (from the penalty spot) and John Hartson put the visitors two up before de Boer replied for Rangers in the second half of the game.

Rangers 0 Celtic 1 League Championship, October 2003

Prior to this first Old Firm game of the season, Rangers were sitting at the top of the table with a 100% record, two points ahead of Celtic. However, John Hartson's 50th club goal meant that the top two swapped position with both psychological and point advantage to Celtic at this early stage of the campaign.

Celtic 3 Rangers 0 League Championship, January 2004

In one of the most one-sided Celtic/Rangers derby clashes for some considerable time, the league leaders moved eleven points clear following goals from Stilian Petrov, Stanislav Varga and Alan Thompson.

Celtic 1 Rangers 0 Scottish Cup, March 2004

With fellow strikers Chris Sutton and John Hartson both injured, it was Henrik Larsson (with his 14th Old Firm goal for Celtic) who ended the season prematurely for the current holders of the Scottish domestic treble.

Rangers 1 Celtic 2 League Championship, March 2004

Although the score perhaps suggested otherwise, this was a comfortable victory for the visitors who were two goals ahead (Larsson and Thompson) and well in control before Rangers pulled one back near the end of the ninety minutes.

Celtic 1 Rangers 0 League Championship, May 2004

Chris Sutton's superb last minute 'Goal of the Season' candidate ensured a clean sweep of Old Firm victories in the 2003/04 campaign. After a relatively even first half, Celtic completely dominated the second period and created chance after chance before that quite astonishing late strike from the Scottish PFA Player of the Year.

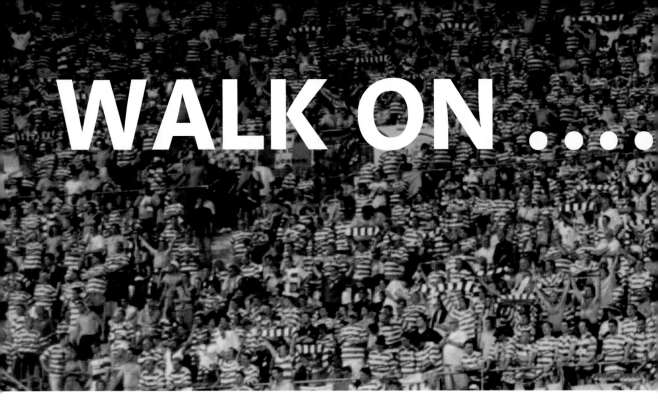

WALK ON . . . .

Even after one of the hottest summers for many a long year, the sun continued to shine on Martin O'Neill and his Celtic side throughout most of Season 2003/04 with League Championship number 39 the prize at the end of a most marvellous campaign. This is the story of another unforgettable chapter in the history of Celtic Football Club.

AUGUST 2003

9.8.03: The first championship encounter of the new campaign began with a journey over the Forth to Dunfermline, Fife in what was to become the final game played on grass at East End Park before the controversial synthetic surface was laid down. With Chris Sutton and John Hartson both missing (suspended and injured respectively), Shaun Maloney was paired up front with Henrik Larsson but neither striker managed to break the stalemate and the ninety minutes ended 0-0. Two facts: it was the first time that Celtic had failed to score in 57 matches and Dunfermline's first point against the Glasgow side since Jimmy Calderwood had arrived as manager in December 1999. As defending champions Rangers had won 4-0 at home to Kilmarnock, Celtic found themselves two points behind after the opening faltering steps of a rather long journey.

THE SPL CHAMPIONSHIP

16.8.03: One week later, Dundee United were the Celtic Park visitors and a crowd of nearly 56,700 spectators (including VIP fan Billy Connelly) witnessed a masterful display of green and white magic with the Tayside outfit quite simply outclassed in all departments. An early Shaun Maloney goal set the ball rolling before Didier Agathe and Alan Thompson (with a penalty) made it 3-0 leading up to the break. Second half strikes from Jackie McNamara and Henrik Larsson completed a 5-0 rout over Ian McCall's Tannadice side but, with both Larsson and Stanislav Varga hitting woodwork during that forty-five minute period, the victory margin could have been even greater.

23.8.03: With summer temperatures still soaring, a short lunchtime trip across Glasgow to the Maryhill Riviera of Firhill was next on the league agenda. Under a blazing noon sun, the anticipated hard game certainly materialised with Grady of Partick Thistle equalising midway through the first half after Paul Lambert's early strike had given his side the lead. All three hard fought points were secured, however, when Alan Thompson netted from the penalty spot (following a foul on Stilian Petrov) just before the interval. After the ninety minutes had come and gone, the visiting fans agreed that it had taken a real battling performance by their team to achieve this close victory.

30.8.03: Seven days on at the end of the month, it was a case of 'two-in-a-row' with the delighted Celtic Park faithful once again being treated to another high five of goals for consecutive home league games. Larsson (with a hat-trick), Shaun Maloney and Alan Thompson (right on

CAMPAIGN OF SEASON 2003/04

the final whistle after a first half penalty miss) did all the damage in the clash with Livingston. With Rangers not playing until the following day, the 'Bhoys' moved to the top of the SPL for the first time that season - even although it was only for a day or so!

SEPTEMBER 2003

13.9.03: Because of a traffic accident on the A9, the start of the away clash with Dundee was delayed for half an hour. However, when the game finally did manage to get underway, it took Celtic less than ten minutes to find the net. With both Johan Mjallby and Joos Valgaeren absent through injury, it was another defender (in the massive shape of 2002/03 Player of the Year Bobo Balde) who stole the show. His early goal, a crashing eighth-minute header from Stephen Crainey's free-kick, was enough to secure victory even although Celts were unfairly reduced to ten men midway through the first half following Didier Agathe's dismissal. This was subsequently viewed by most observers as a miscarriage of football justice. In truth, the Dark Blues, who had not beaten Celtic at Dens Park for fifteen years, rarely threatened and keeper Magnus Hedman did not have a shot to save in the entire ninety minutes of the game.

20.9.03: After celebrating his 32nd birthday on September 20, Henrik Larsson was gifted a card (yellow – for diving) by referee Iain Brines the following day when Terry Butcher's Motherwell visited the east end of Glasgow. After a blank forty-five, the Swede's header (goal number seven for the season so far) opened the scoring early in the second

period before Chris Sutton and Shaun Maloney made it three to complete another excellent day's work at the office.

27.9.03: September's last league game was a trip east along the M8 to Scotland's capital to face Hibernian at Easter Road where, for the first time since the start of the championship campaign, Celtic conceded the opening goal. The home side's lead (a little 'Sunshine on Leith' perhaps) was, however, short-lived and Doumbe's 38th minute strike was cancelled out just two minutes later when Alan Thompson converted from the penalty spot after Stilian Petrov had been brought down in the box. Then, with the second half barely commenced, a delightful flowing move (involving Varga, Maloney and Larsson) ended with Henrik finding the net for a 2-1 Celtic lead. Although Bobo Balde was red carded with some thirty minutes of play still remaining, extra-man Hibernian could not build on their numerical advantage and all three points were soon heading out of town and back west.

OCTOBER 2003

4.10.03: Prior to the first Old Firm clash of the 2003/04 campaign, Rangers sat at the top of the SPL with twenty-one points (two ahead of Celtic in second place) with the Ibrox club also additionally having scored more goals – 26 as opposed to Celtic's total of 18. Martin O'Neill's side, however, had never lost the initial Old Firm joust in any season since the Irishman arrived at the club (wins of 6-2 and 2-0 as well as a 3-3 draw to his name) and, once again, a fascinating game was in prospect.

As it happened, it proved to be somewhat less than a classic encounter but John Hartson's fiftieth goal in the colours (a wicked deflection off Georgian defender Khizanishvili right at the beginning of the second half) meant that it was memorable to one side of the great divide and his team, therefore, replaced Rangers at the top in the championship race. Interestingly, Celtic had now won the last three Old Firm league games by a single goal and the Welshman had scored in all of them.

18.10.03: Much was expected of Hearts (the perceived 'third force in Scottish Football') prior to their Glasgow visit in mid October but, like so many others that season, the Tynecastle outfit were simply broken and brushed aside as Celtic went on the rampage, handing out a real thrashing. Midfielder Liam Miller opened the scoring before ten minutes play had lapsed and, by half time, it was another three courtesy of Stamp (an own goal), Larsson and Varga - the Slovak's first-ever Celtic goal. Miller's second, shortly after the break, completed the 5-0 rout. Astonishingly,

CAMPAIGN OF SEASON 2003/04

in the following four league outings, the fans would witness the bulging of opposition nets no less than nineteen times as Celts continued to storm ahead in the championship.

25.10.03: Despite having a fair amount of first half possession, Aberdeen still found themselves three goals behind when the referee blew at the end of the opening forty-five minutes. A Larsson brace (his second was a glorious twenty-five yard free kick) and a Chris Sutton penalty did all the damage in that first period. The Swede (different class as always) completed his hat-trick soon after the restart and thus moved ahead of both Arveladze (Rangers) and Novo (Dundee) in the SPL chart for goalscorers. Final score: 4-0.

NOVEMBER 2003

1.11.03: Rugby Park was the next port of call on league business and, for the second time on the road last season, kick-off was once again delayed. However, there was no delay in the performance of head 'Bhoy' Chris Sutton and the Englishman ended the Kilmarnock outing with a hat-trick (which included two penalties) to his name. Hartson and Maloney were the other scorers on a day when Celtic's final four goals all arrived in the last fifteen minutes of play in a game that seemed, at one stage, to be heading for the 'close encounter' category.

8.11.03: Speaking of close calls, it seemed that one was on the cards at Celtic Park the following week when a well organised Dunfermline side were only one down (John Hartson - first half) with, again, only some fifteen minutes left on the clock. To manager Jimmy Calderwood's despair, however, it was a case of lightning striking twice and Hartson, Ross Wallace (the 18-year-old's first competitive goal for the club), Varga and Larsson all contributed to make it another famous five for the fans. Incidentally, keeper Rab Douglas was back 'between the sticks' for the first time since the game with Partick Thistle in late August.

22.11.03: With both Douglas and McNamara missing from the starting line-up on Tayside two weeks later, the team was Scot-free for only the second time in the league campaign. Although manager Ian McCall's Dundee United side played far better than when the teams last met in August, the 'Arabs' still saw the ball hit the back of their net no less than five times - with three from hat-trick hombre Sutton and two from Larsson making up the visitors' grand total that day.

THE SPL CHAMPIONSHIP

29.11.03: For November's last encounter, Partick Thistle made the very wet journey (to another deluge?) from west to east Glasgow in the knowledge that their sum total of two league points was the same number of points that Celtic had dropped this far in the championship. On that basis alone, it was surprising in the extreme when the visitors went ahead early (through Grady) but the 'Hoops' replied via Larsson to square the first half spoils. Chris Sutton, the previous week's hat-trick hero, grabbed a double after the break to ensure a 3-1 victory. To their credit, Thistle had just achieved the best result to date (in campaign 2003/04) of any Premier League side at the intimidating fortress that is Castle Celtic.

DECEMBER 2003

6.12.03: Prior to Celtic's early December visit to the City Stadium, Livingston had been beaten only once in seven games on their home turf this season so far with even champions Rangers failing to retreat to Govan with victory spoils. Although the east of Scotland side managed to keep their high flying visitors at bay in the first period (despite Celtic's six corners in just sixteen minutes!), second half strikes from Chris Sutton and Alan Thompson kept the league leaders five points ahead at the top of the table.

13.12.03: Dundee, it must be said, made a real game of it when they travelled to Glasgow the following week and created several good chances. After Larsson's left foot strike opened the scoring on the fifteen minute mark, ex-Celt Kevin Fotheringham replied with a thunderous drive from the edge of the box to make it 1-1. But, in the

CAMPAIGN OF SEASON 2003/04

next forty-five, Bobo Balde's close-range header and substitute John Kennedy's strike (also from close-in) answered all the questions before Mair claimed a second for Jim Duffy's side in injury time.

21.12.03: Fir Park, Motherwell is one of those venues where any victory usually falls into the 'hard-fought' category and this was certainly the case on a very cold Sunday afternoon in Lanarkshire. The home side responded well after John Hartson had given Celts the lead in just three minutes but Rab Douglas, with a marvellous one-handed stop from an Adams penalty, kept his team in front. After the interval, the 'Bhoys' began to dominate the fixture and, in due course, sealed victory some twenty minutes before the final whistle courtesy of Alan Thompson's beautifully judged free-kick which curled over the defensive wall and into the back of the net. Merry Christmas, indeed! Earlier in the game, Henrik Larsson had been controversially booked for diving by referee Underhill, bringing back memories of a similar yellow card offence for the Swede when the same teams met on league duty back in September.

27.12.03: With Hibernian (in the CIS Cup) the only Scottish outfit to have beaten Celtic, the post Christmas clash at Celtic park had more than a passing interest to many neutrals who wondered if Bobby Williamson's side could do it again. Despite the set-back of Chris Sutton's early goal, the Easter Road outfit competed well in the first half but the dismissal

of Riordan just before the interval (for a scything tackle on Jackie McNamara) completely changed the complexion of the game. John Hartson made it two almost immediately and then, in the second forty-five, goals from Sutton, Hartson, Larsson and Petrov meant that the team's astonishing spree of five goals in six different league outings had now been topped with one 'six of the best' caning.

JANUARY 2004

3.1.04: Eight points adrift, defending champions Rangers headed across Glasgow for the second Old Firm meeting of the season knowing that only a win would suffice but, in truth, they never matched their hosts in any department, shape or form and Celtic ran out the most convincing of 3-0 winners. Stilian Petrov's first half headed goal (which struck both posts before crossing the line) separated the teams at the break. Following the interval, Stanislav Varga and Alan Thompson (whose set-pieces had caused mayhem throughout the Ibrox rearguard the whole afternoon) added their names to the roll of honour. Celts were now eleven points and, astonishingly, thirty goals ahead of their greatest rivals in the SPL stakes. No wonder many neutrals felt that the destination of the 2003/04 SPL title had already been decided.

18.1.04: In the first of difficult consecutive away games, Celtic made the M8 trip to Tynecastle for what ultimately turned out to be an explosive fixture with Hearts. Although all three points were made safe after Stilian Petrov's first-half strike between the legs of young keeper Gordon, the match's other main talking points (which filled the newspaper back pages for some days) revolved around both missile-throwing and off-the-ball controversy. Not to mention the matter of ten yellow cards split equally between the teams in a clash that saw fire meet fire! Incidentally, this was defender Bobo Balde's last outing for some time as he headed off south to warmer days to play for his country in the African Nations Cup.

24.1.04: Regardless of Aberdeen's improvement in form during the previous few weeks (just one defeat in their seven most recent games), the Pittodrie side duly met the Celtic fate that greeted all SPL teams since the second championship outing of the current campaign. Captain of Bulgaria Stilian Petrov claimed the opener - for the third league match in a row - before Henrik Larsson (with his first January goal) made it two before the break. Then, with half an hour of play still remaining, new signing Stephen Pearson scored his side's third and his first Celtic

CAMPAIGN OF SEASON 2003/04

goal since joining from Motherwell. When Steve Tosh grabbed a consolation effort after this to give Aberdeen a little northern light, it was remarkably only the eighth goal that the visitors had lost in twenty-one league matches. Indeed, Tosh's Finnish team-mate Markus Heikkinen had commented that this Celtic side was stronger than the Italian Serie A teams that the player had faced previously in his career.

31.1.04: On the wettest of wet days. Kilmarnock, who had not won any of their previous six league games, reached the half time break at Celtic park without conceding a goal. In the second period, however, they were just swamped! Having been pushed further forward at the start of the second forty-five, Didier Agathe made the breakthrough with his second league goal of the current campaign. After that, it was simply a case of how many with Hartson (a double of two headed goals), Larsson and Pearson all contributing to a final score of 5-1. Although Skora's late strike offered a little consolation, Kilmarnock returned to Ayrshire in the knowledge that it was now an incredible forty-nine years since they had celebrated victory at Celtic Park.

FEBRUARY 2004

11.2.04: For this midweek fixture, Celtic returned to the only ground where they had dropped championship points so far in the current campaign. Of course, since the last game against Dunfermline at East End Park (0-0, August 2003), the Fifers had laid down their controversial plastic pitch and, understandably, many teams struggled on the synthetic surface. How would Celtic cope? Although the home side opened the scoring through their little Irish striker Hunt in twenty minutes, the latter question had been well and truly answered before the interval. Larsson set the ball rolling with a headed equaliser (three minutes after Dunfermline's opener) before Varga and Henrik (again) made it 3-1 for the visitors at half-time. Interestingly, all three Celtic goals had been headed home from superb Alan Thompson balls into the box. In the second period, it was the Englishman himself who made it four with a superb free-kick after Petrov had been fouled. Noting that the league leaders had registered their 100th goal of the season, it was left to Dunfermline to ponder on a fifteen year winless sequence against Celtic.

14.2.04: With closest rivals Rangers only managing a draw against Aberdeen at Pittodrie in the lunchtime televised game, the Hoops had the opportunity to increase their lead at the top of the table by beating Dundee United at Celtic Park. After a blank first-half, the visitors went

ahead on the hour mark and Celtic's astonishing run of successive victories seemed to be in real danger of ending as the game entered its final phase with, as yet, no reply from Martin O'Neill's team. Certainly, there would be no St. Valentine's Day Massacre! Then, with just nine minutes left, substitute Shaun Maloney netted from close range after being picked out by Chris Sutton. Barely one minute on from the equaliser, Celts were awarded a penalty (after Duff was adjudged to have fouled Petrov in the box) and Sutton made no mistake from the spot, finally ending United's stubborn resistance. After twenty-four games played, Celtic were now thirteen points ahead of the defending champions.

22.2.04: Prior to the start of the fixture against relegation-threatened Partick Thistle, the Firhill side languished at the bottom of the SPL with just twelve league points to their name. With Celtic totally dominating today's game from start to finish, an increase in that points total was only a remote possibility. After Chris Sutton had opened the scoring with a flying header from close-range, Stan Varga made it two (with another header), six minutes before the half-time whistle. Both goals

had been created by the deadly left-foot of Alan Thompson. In the second period, Sutton doubled his tally with a converted penalty (his seventh successful penalty out of seven) before former Celt Gerry Britton pulled one back for the Jags. Then, in the final ten minutes of the game, defender Varga claimed his side's fourth goal of the afternoon (and his seventh of the season) with yet another header. In addition to another three most welcome championship points, Celtic had now surpassed

CAMPAIGN OF SEASON 2003/04

Morton's long-standing record of twenty-three consecutive league victories which the Greenock club had established some forty years previously, way back in Season 1963/64. Many neutrals were of the opinion that the current Celtic side was the best to wear those famous colours for many years.

29.2.04: Visitors Livingston (minus, of course, on-loan and in form striker David Fernandez who watched the game from the stand) actually started well but it was Stephen Pearson who opened the scoring in just twelve minutes with Celtic's 50th home SPL goal of the season. Then, following an Alan Thompson free-kick, Chris Sutton was next on the score sheet (with his 24th in all competitions) before Lilley pulled one back just before the interval. By this time, the home fans were in a rather joyous mood as news had filtered through from Tannadice that defending champions Rangers were 2-0 down to Dundee United. Early in the second half, a delightful right-foot shot from Thompson made it three before, minutes later, Henrik Larsson added his name to the list of scorers after an indirect free-kick had been awarded in the Livingston box. A converted Thompson penalty late-on ensured a repeat of the 5-1 August score when Livingston last visited at the start of the 2003/04 league campaign. Celtic were now a massive sixteen points ahead in the title race with the crown now well within their grasp.

MARCH 2004

14.3.04: Three days after the mighty Barcelona were beaten at Celtic Park in the UEFA Cup tournament, Terry Butcher's Motherwell (sitting proudly in the top six) became the first SPL side to take points off Celtic since Dunfermline had managed a 0-0 draw way back in August 2003 on the first day of the campaign. With Douglas, Lennon and Thompson all injured and Larsson, Agathe and McNamara on the bench, visiting skipper Derek Adams (at odds of 40-1 with the bookmakers to be the first goalscorer) had given his side a 1-0 lead before the forty-five minute break. Although Paul Lambert hit the post right at the beginning of the second period, it was Henrik Larsson (in his new, rarely seen guise as 'Super Sub') who finally scored for Celtic when he came off the bench and netted from close range to ensure a share of the points. Late-on, it could have been a case of all three for the SPL leaders if Pearson's thunderous, bar-rattling drive had been just a couple of inches lower.

THE SPL CHAMPIONSHIP

17.3.04: Only one goal separated Celtic and Dundee on their two previous clashes this season when results of 3-2 and 1-0 were recorded in December and September respectively. With another close tussle in prospect when the teams met at Dens Park three days after the Motherwell clash, the usual suspects of Larsson, Agathe, Thompson, Lennon and McNamara all returned to the starting line-up for this BBC televised game. Ten minutes before the interval, with both sides having created chances, the visitors took the lead when Stilian Petrov claimed his eighth goal of the season following a lung-bursting 60 yard run by Pearson. It should have been two shortly after but Larsson's conversion was wrongly flagged offside. However, in the second half, the Swede would not be denied and duly claimed his 30th of the season after keeper Speroni had blocked his first penalty box effort before Dundee substitute Kneissl made it 1-2 right at the end. From a statistical point of view, Henrik Larsson had now totalled 231 career goals for Celtic, thus equalling the tally of club legend and 'Lisbon Lion' Stevie Chalmers. Only

Jimmy McGrory and Bobby Lennox were still ahead of the Swede in that particular chart.

21.3.04: After their disappointing display in the final of the CIS Insurance Cup at Hampden the previous week, Hibernian were naturally hoping to put on more of a show for their fans when Celtic came calling for this Sunday TV showdown. Although Bobby Williamson's side started the game well, it was the visitors who took the lead after just 18 minutes when Didier Agathe met Pearson's low cross at the back post to net past Andersson in goal. Ten minutes before the interval, following a Lambert through ball, the Hibernian keeper was more than a little to blame when

CAMPAIGN OF SEASON 2003/04

he delayed and allowed Henrik Larsson to steal the ball from him and double Celtic's advantage. Early in the second period, the Swede claimed another when he buried through the keeper's legs before Agathe claimed his brace with an angled drive under Andersson near the end of the afternoon's game.

28.3.04: Just three days after his heroic deeds against Barcelona in the UEFA Cup, stand-in keeper David Marshall was voted BBC Man of the Match following his tremendous display in the 2-1 away win over Rangers. With Celtic a goal ahead courtesy of Henrik Larsson's penalty box header (the Swede's fourth Ibrox goal and his fifteenth in Old Firm clashes), the young stopper was called into action and produced sensational saves from a wicked deflection off Varga and a net-bound header from full back Hutton as Rangers poured forward in search of an equaliser. The points were secured early in the second period when Alan Thompson netted after Klos had blocked Stephen Pearson's initial effort on goal. Although the home side pulled one back when substitute Thompson headed home, Celtic ended the game deserved winners. They were now an astonishing nineteen points ahead in the title race, with another six required to be officially crowned champions. Incidentally, Martin O'Neill's side had become the first Celtic team since the 1971/72 period to have won five consecutive Old Firm games.

APRIL 2004

3.4.04: With only 150 seconds of normal time left and Hearts 2-0 ahead, it looked as if Celtic's proud unbeaten home record (which encompassed an astonishing 76 Scottish and European games) was about to come to an end. Once again, however, Martin O'Neill's team lived the 'never knowing it is beaten' cliché and netted twice to draw level before the referee blew for full-time. Visitors Hearts had started well against a Celtic side missing both Lennon and Petrov and deservedly went ahead through McKenna in twenty minutes. In the second period, with less than fifteen minutes remaining, striker De Vries doubled their advantage and it looked all over for the home side but Chris Sutton pulled one back (with 88 minutes on the clock) before Didier Agathe raised the roof with a left-footed equaliser right at the end of the regulation period.

18.4.04: Following Rangers' mid-week draw with Livingston, Celtic now required just one more victory (or three points) to regain the SPL title and domestic championship number 39. As the fates would have it, the next port of call on league duty was Rugby Park, Kilmarnock, the scene

THE SPL CHAMPIONSHIP

of the previous year's final day heartbreak. However, the circumstances prior to the game this time round were somewhat different – to say the least! With Alan Thompson out injured, Celtic began with seven of the team that featured here on that disappointing day in May 2003. After the home side had a 'goal' disallowed early-on, it was the visitors who went ahead after half an hour when, following Henrik Larsson's head flick, player-of-the-year contender Stilian Petrov burst through the Kilmarnock defence to steer the ball past Meldrum. Although both sides created additional chances in each half, this proved to be the only goal of the game and the festivities began for what Martin O'Neill suggested was the most rewarding triumph of his managerial career to date. The SPL Championship Trophy was back at Celtic Park!

21.4.04: This midweek re-arranged fixture against Aberdeen surprisingly brought to an end Celtic's astonishing 77 game run of unbeaten fixtures at home that stretched way back to August 2001. Although Henrik Larsson opened the scoring after quarter of an hour with his 36th goal of the season (and Celtic's 99th in the 2003/04 SPL campaign), Aberdeen equalised in the second half through substitute Prunty, a former Celtic reserve, before Australian striker David Zdrilic slotted home the winner in injury time for an unexpected conclusion to the game.

25.4.04: Celtic travelled to Tynecastle for the first of their remaining five championship fixtures minus the talents of Chris Sutton, Alan Thompson, Jackie McNamara and Stephen Pearson. Making his debut in the side was 18-year-old Aiden McGeady who, indeed, opened the scoring in twenty minutes with a driving penalty box shot that went in off the post. Although Hearts substitute De Vries equalised in the second half, the game belonged to young McGeady and his standing ovation from the Celtic legions (when he left the park with some twenty minutes remaining) was richly deserved – as was his BBC Man of the Match award after the game.

MAY 2004

2.5.04: Cup final opponents Dunfermline became the second team in less than two weeks to win at Celtic Park when goals from Nicholson and Dempsey cancelled out one from Larsson and ensured a Pars victory in

CAMPAIGN OF SEASON 2003/04

Glasgow for the first time since August 1997. Celtic, it must be noted, were without McNamara, Agathe, Balde and Petrov. After the game, however, the events of the previous ninety minutes were soon forgotten as both fans and team celebrated following the presentation of the SPL trophy. Once again, this part of Glasgow was a veritable sea of green and white!

8.5.04: The first half of the final Old Firm clash of the season was certainly evenly balanced between the combatants. The second period told a different story however as Celtic totally dominated the whole forty-five minutes, creating but failing to take the numerous chances to win the game. Just when it seemed as if there would be no scoring before full time, Chris Sutton produced something quite magical. Taking Larsson's pass, the big striker held off defender de Boer before chipping Klos from distance for an astonishing match-winner. Celtic had now equalled Rangers' record (from the 1963/64 campaign) of five Old Firm victories in one season.

12.5.04: The venue for Celtic's penultimate league game of the campaign was a short distance along the motorway to Motherwell. In what turned out to be a somewhat fiery encounter, the players of both sides were so totally committed that referee Rowbotham seemed to be in a war zone at times despite the fact that the season was virtually over with little at stake. Craig Beattie equalised for Celtic (after Clarkson had put the home side ahead in the second half) and the game ended 1-1 with a pitch invasion by the home support after the final whistle.

16.5.04: Another marvellous league campaign for Martin O'Neill's men drew to a close with Dundee United the Glasgow visitors. With Tayside keeper Gallacher in fine form, it looked as if Henrik Larsson's final competitive game at Celtic Park would not have the required fairy-tale ending but, as on so many previous occasions, the Swede did not disappoint his adoring public. Two strikes in the last ten minutes of the game (one of which was a trademark header) lifted his Celtic career tally to an astonishing 240 goals in just seven seasons, with the Scottish Cup Final against Dunfermline still to come. As they say, a player in a million!

THE SPL CHAMPIONSHIP
CAMPAIGN OF SEASON 2003/04

CELTIC IN EUROPE QUIZ
SEASON 2003/04

1. Who were Celtic's first European opponents last season?

2. In the next qualifying round of the Champions League, Celtic beat the champions of which country?

3. Why was the above away game stopped temporarily early in the second half?

4. Henrik Larsson set a new European goalscoring record during the above encounter. What was his goal tally after this game?

5. Can you remember the three other teams in Celtic's Champions League group of Season 2003/04?

6. Who scored Celtic's first goal in the above Champions League group?

7. Chris Sutton was top scorer for Celts after the six games. True or false?

8. Which of the six Champions League encounters attracted the biggest crowd?

9. Whose goal beat Barcelona at Celtic Park in the Uefa Cup tie of 11th March?

10. Why were both Chris Sutton and Alan Thompson missing from the April Uefa Cup return-leg with Villarreal in Spain?

ANSWERS ON PAGE 61

NAME THE CELT

FILL IN THE NAME OF THE MISSING CELT FROM THIS SELECTION OF SEASON 2003/04 FOOTBALL HEADLINES. THE CLUE IS IN THE DATE!

IF YOU DON'T RECOGNISE THE DATE - THE PICTURE MIGHT HELP

1 '............... LEADS IN FIVE-STAR SHOWCASE' 23.11.03

'BATTLE-SCARRED DEFENCE IS GIVEN THE .... OF LIFE' 5.10.03 **2**

3 '............... THE LYON TAMER' 1.10.03

'STUNNED BY AN ACT OF ....' 18.9.03 **4**

5 '................ GLIDES CELTS INTO CRUISE CONTROL' 3.11.03

'.............GOING WILL BE LIKE LOSING ONE OF THE FAMILY' 18.1.04 **6**

7 '................ CAPITAL PUNISHMENT' 8.2.04

'HEARTACHE AGAIN FOR ....' 3.3.04 **8**

9 '................ RULE' 26.3.04

'...............EXTENDS IBROX SUFFERING' 9.5.04 **10**

ANSWERS ON PAGE 61

54

IF YOU KNOW
THE HISTORY

MANAGERS AND WINNERS

WILLIAM MALEY

WILLIAM MALEY (1897-1940)
16 League Championships, 14 Scottish Cups plus Glasgow
Exhibition Trophy (1902) and Empire Exhibition Trophy

JIMMY McSTAY

JIMMY McSTAY (1940-1945)
Victory in Europe Cup (1945)

JIMMY McGRORY

JIMMY McGRORY (1945-1965)
1 League Championship, 2 Scottish Cups, 2 League Cups
plus St. Mungo Cup (1951) and Coronation Cup (1953)

JOCK STEIN

JOCK STEIN (1965-1978)
10 League Championships, 8 Scottish Cups, 6 League Cups
and the European Cup (1967)

BILLY McNEILL

BILLY McNEILL (1978-1983)
3 League Championships, 1 Scottish Cup and 1 League Cup

DAVID HAY

DAVID HAY (1983-1987)
1 League Championship and 1 Scottish Cup

TOMMY BURNS

BILLY McNEILL (1987-1991)
1 League Championship and 2 Scottish Cups

TOMMY BURNS (1994-1997)
1 Scottish Cup

WIM JANSEN

WIM JANSEN (1997-1998)
1 League Championship and 1 League Cup

KENNY DALGLISH

KENNY DALGLISH (Interim Head Coach 2000)
1 League Cup

MARTIN O'NEILL

MARTIN O'NEILL (2000-   )
3 League Championships, 2 Scottish Cups and 1 League Cup

FROM THE TROPHY ROOMS

REAL MADRID SILVER CABIN 1980

Following the famous League Championship success of Season 1978/79 (the title was secured at Celtic Park in late May courtesy of a stunning 4-2 win over Old Firm rivals Rangers), the European Cup beckoned once again in the autumn of 1979. Despite losing 1-0 away to Partizan Tirana of Albania in the first round, first leg, Celtic were convincing 4-1 winners in the return Glasgow encounter. After the Irish of Dundalk were beaten 3-2 on aggregate in the next round, it was a truly mouth-watering prospect - European legends Real Madrid in the quarter final!

Simply awesome in the first game in Glasgow, Celts played outstanding football throughout the regulation ninety minutes. Although it was still 0-0 at half time, second period goals from George McCluskey and John Doyle (a rare headed strike by the tenacious winger) ensured a two goal cushion before the daunting prospect of a trip to the majestic Bernabeu Stadium of Spain's capital city two weeks later.

In truth, the return leg started well for Celtic who really should have scored early-on but missed a golden opportunity that may just have booked their place in the semi-final. Then, maybe inevitably, Real began to take control and, with a combination of both forceful and skilful play, eventually secured a 3-0 quarter-final triumph. They had, however, survived a strong penalty appeal against them (for handling), in addition to an almost 'own goal' scenario by defender Pirri.

This magnificent and unique piece of silver was presented to the club by their Spanish opponents to mark the occasion.

5.3.80   CELTIC 2 REAL MADRID 0
McCluskey (52 mins)
Doyle (74 mins)

Celtic: Latchford, Sneddon, McGrain, Aitken, McAdam, MacDonald, MacLeod, Provan, Lennox, McCluskey and Doyle.

19.3.80   REAL MADRID 3 CELTIC 0

Celtic: Latchford, Sneddon, McAdam, MacDonald, McGrain, Provan, Aitken, Doyle, MacLeod, McCluskey (Burns) and Lennox.

CELTIC – THE HONOURS

Scottish League Championships (39 in total)

1892/93, 1893/94, 1895/96, 1897/98, 1904/05, 1905/06, 1906/07, 1907/08, 1908/09, 1909/10, 1913/14, 1914/15, 1915/16, 1916/17, 1918/19, 1921/22, 1925/26, 1935/36, 1937/38, 1953/54, 1965/66, 1966/67, 1967/68, 1968/69, 1969/70, 1970/71, 1971/72, 1972/73, 1973/74, 1976/77, 1978/79, 1980/81, 1981/82, 1985/86, 1987/88, 1997/98, 2000/01, 2001/02, 2003/04.

Scottish Cups (32)

1892, 1899, 1900, 1904, 1907, 1908, 1911, 1912, 1914, 1923, 1925, 1927, 1931, 1933, 1937, 1951, 1954, 1965, 1967, 1969, 1971, 1972, 1974, 1975, 1977, 1980, 1985, 1988, 1989, 1995, 2001, 2004.

Scottish League Cups (12)

1956, 1957, 1965, 1966, 1967, 1968, 1969, 1974, 1982, 1997, 2000, 2001.

European Cup 1967

Uefa Cup Runners up 2003

Coronation Cup 1953

St. Mungo Cup 1951

Victory in Europe Cup 1945

Empire Exhibition Trophy 1938

Scottish League Commemorative Shield 1904/05 – 1909/10

Glasgow Exhibition Cup 1902

QUIZ ANSWERS

WHAT THE PAPERS SAID

1. Celtic go 11 points clear of Rangers at the top of the Premier League after a comprehensive 3-0 early January victory at Celtic Park.
2. Chris Sutton claims a double in the 6-0 league thrashing of Hibernian.
3. Celtic claim their 21st consecutive SPL victory of the season when Kilmarnock are crushed 5-1 on the last day of January.
4. John Hartson's first goal of the season as Rangers are beaten 1-0 at Ibrox.
5. A marvellous penalty save by Rab Douglas at Fir Park against Motherwell.
6. Henrik Larsson's goal in the Scottish Cup tie with Rangers effectively ends the Ibrox side's season.
7. Celtic's fabulous performance against Barcelona in Spain ensures progress to the quarter-final of the Uefa Cup.
8. Celtic are SPL Champions for Season 2003/04.
9. After a sensational debut against Hearts, young Scot Aiden McGeady confirmed his desire to play international football for Ireland.
10. In his final league game at Celtic Park, Henrik Larsson claims both goals in the 2-1 win over Dundee United.

CELTIC AND THE DOMESTIC CUPS QUIZ – SEASON 2003/04

1. First Division Ross County.
2. David Marshall.
3. 2-0 – Jamie Smith and Craig Beattie.
4. Stanislav Varga.
5. Nine – both Hartley and Maybury had been dismissed.
6. Stilian Petrov.
7. True – they were both injured.
8. Chris Sutton.
9. False – it was Stilian Petrov.
10. Jackie McNamara.

KING OF GOALS HENRIK LARSSON QUIZ

1. Feyenoord.
2. Wim Jansen.
3. His misplaced pass found Hibernian's Chic Charnley who then netted the winner.
4. False – Celtic lifted both the League Championship and the League Cup in Season 1997/98.
5. 38 goals in 48 games.
6. Henrik suffered a horrendous leg injury in the French city of Lyon.
7. False – it was actually an incredible tally of 53 goals.
8. Charlie Nicholas.
9. He netted a hat-trick.
10. Bobby Lennox (273 goals) and Jimmy McGrory with an incredible total of 468 goals.

CHAMPIONS QUIZ

1. Shaun Maloney and Henrik Larsson.
2. Dundee United (5-0, 16.8.03), Livingston (5-1, 30.8.03), Hearts (5-0, 18.10.03), Kilmarnock (5-0, 1.11.03), Dunfermline (5-0, 8.11.03) and Dundee United (5-1, 22.11.03).
3. Henrik Larsson.
4. Henrik Larsson in the August 5-1 demolition of Livingston.
5. Stilian Petrov in the games with Rangers, Hearts and Aberdeen.
6. He left the country for international duty in the African Nations Cup.
7. 4-1 with goals from Larsson (2), Varga and Thompson.
8. Stephen Pearson in the 5-1 victory over Livingston in late February.
9. Stilian Petrov.
10. Celtic's 77-match unbeaten home run ended at the hands of Aberdeen.

SEASON 2003/04 OLD FIRM QUIZ

1. Celtic won 1-0 at Ibrox.
2. John Hartson.
3. Stilian Petrov's diving header hit both posts before crossing the line.
4. Jackie McNamara.
5. Eleven points.
6. False – it was his 50th Celtic goal.
7. Henrik Larsson.
8. 15.
9. Alan Thompson.
10. Chris Sutton.

CELTIC IN EUROPE QUIZ – SEASON 2003/04

1. FBK Kaunas of Lithuania in the Champions League second qualifying round.
2. Hungary.
3. A water sprinkler burst near the centre circle.
4. 31 goals.
5. Bayern Munich, Lyon and Anderlecht.
6. Alan Thompson.
7. True - with three goals.
8. The Celtic Park clash with Bayern Munich was watched by a crowd of 59,506.
9. Alan Thompson.
10. Sutton was injured and Thompson was suspended.

NAME THE CELT QUIZ

1. SUTTON - Chris scores a hat-trick as Dundee United are demolished 5-1 at Tannadice in the SPL campaign.
2. CHRIS – With Bobo Balde suspended, Chris Sutton is quite magnificent at the heart of the Celtic defence as Rangeres are beaten 1-0 at Ibrox.
3. LARSSON – Henrik silences the Lyon doubters with a superb display in the 2-0 Champions League encounter.
4. MAGNUS – a late lapse by Magnus Hedman in Munich as Celtic lose 2-1 in the Champions League.
5. SUTTON - Three of the five Celtic goals at Rugby Park have Chris Sutton's name on them.
6. HENRIK – Neil Lennon speaking about the summer departure of Henrik Larsson.
7. PETROV'S – The Bulgarian's two goals killed off Hearts in the Edinburgh Scottish Cup tie.
8. HARTSON – John Hartson's season ends prematurely for the second successive year with another back problem.
9. MARSHALL – Young goalkeeper David Marshall is simply magnificent in the Nou Camp Uefa Cup game with Celtic.
10. SUTTON – Chris Sutton's stunning late goal in the last Old Firm clash of the season.

BANK OF
PREMIERLEA

CHAMPIONS
2003 - 2004